What should I tell you?

A mother's final words to her infant son

Compiled by her sister Jo

self published at
www.printmatters.info

First published April 2008

on

behalf of Jo Middlemiss

by

printmatters,

16 - 18 Swan Street, Brechin, Angus DD9 6EF

2nd edition: April 2008

ISBN 978 0 9559153 0 7

Bought from Jo at the Marie Louise
Health & Wellbeing Day – Green Hotel,
Kinross – 15 October 2009 – 10 Am till Noon.

printed and bound by printmatters

"Pray for me,
As I will for thee,
That we may merrily meet in heaven"

St. Thomas More's farewell to his
daughter Margaret

Foreword & Appreciation

I first thought of this book as I was on a training walk for the Moonwalk Marathon in February 2007. I instantly put the idea to Srini and Francis and they responded immediately and positively. So my first thanks go hugely and absolutely to them. I want to thank them also for the freedom to do as I pleased with my ideas and my interpretation of how things might have been for them. I then went to Kevin Walsh who rescued the tape onto C.D and enthused in the early stages. To Laura Bonthron who painstakingly transcribed the tape. To Bill Sturrock at printmatters for his endless patience; to Avril Nicoll for reading and re reading and gently suggesting and skilful editing; to Jan Ogilvie who typed up all the letters and read and re-read the script; to Kirsten Walker for the wonderful illustrations; to Mary's girls Catherine and Eileen for love and support; to Mia, my beloved sister-in-law who is much much more than that to me, for all her enthusiasm and encouragement; to my wonderful brothers Johnny, Frank, Gerry, Bernard, and their great wives and families; to my unique parents, especially darling Mother, still soldiering on against the odds and of course to my dear husband Andy, our boys and their new families. It's all about LOVE, giving it and receiving it, no matter what. I know that, Maggie knew that and she wanted Francis to know it also, so that the message would go on and on.

My biggest thanks has to be to Maggie herself, whose

thoughtfulness at the time of her most intense suffering has led to such a powerful example of how it is possible to live and to die well. I have often felt that it was she who was holding the pen and keeping me at it when my initial enthusiasm was slipping. I asked myself often "Why are you doing this?" Then I would think about all the people who need help through this precious time of their lives. This is when it is so important to be honest, and when palliative care needs to be of the very best.

I do not think it coincidence that Srini moved from surgery to palliative care, which he now consults in and my own son Thomas, Maggie's Godson, has also chosen palliative care as his speciality. If this book helps in any way to change attitudes around the subject of death, dying and living well all the way through to the next stage, whatever that is, then I shall be truly delighted.

Ways to approach reading this book

Kuala Lumpur, 1982

Just as we were about to set off to Kuala Lumpur for a year, we got devastating news. Far from Maggie's cancer being in remission, it had returned in a rampant fashion, and she was to have her leg amputated immediately. As she was recovering, it became clear that this cancer was not going to be denied. A phone call in the middle of New Year's night told us that there were tumours everywhere. The illness was to be managed now, with palliative care the order of the day.

Maggie had been planning to visit us in Kuala Lumpur, but the advice on that was a very definite negative. I had to stay with my children and was deeply sad. Maggie was my dearest friend, as well as the sister I had shared a room with for 23 years. She was being well supported by other members of the family but I wanted so much to see her.

We were discussing the pros and cons of me leaving the children and going to Canada, when my eldest son's teacher sent for me. She said she was so sorry to hear from Peter about my illness. I explained that it was my sister who was ill not me, but I knew in that moment that my little children did not understand what was going on, and that my distress was distressing them. I took the difficult decision not to disrupt my children's lives, when others were well able to visit and support Maggie. I was on the point of phoning and delivering this message, when

Maggie called to say that she was going to make the trip to Kuala Lumpur. This was so against advice, but Maggie wanted to make a farewell journey - not only to visit me, but also all the friends and relatives who wanted to see her, but were unable to make the trip to Canada.

Maggie had set God a challenge: "If it is the right thing for me to make this journey I want a sign". The next morning she woke up pain-free for the first time in many months. The pain stayed absent until the first class round the world tickets were bought.

Srini and Maggie visited their best man in America. They came to me, and then went on to India, where she met her in-laws for the first and only time. They concluded their journey by visiting family and friends in the United Kingdom. They showed many people that the manner of your death can supersede the awfulness of the loss.

But let me return to Kuala Lumpur, because that is the part of the story I know best. Words cannot portray the excitement I felt on the day that Maggie and Srini were due to arrive. I think I must have prayed night and day that some amazing miracle would occur; faith moves mountains, does it not? Kuala Lumpur airport, chaotic at the best of times, was under some kind of reconstruction. Andy, with an official badge and in uniform, was able to go through with a wheelchair to meet the plane, while I stood in the packed, humid concourse, desperate for my first view of her in over a year. My baby son Oliver was exactly one year old and she had yet to meet him. It was such a relief to see her: thin as a stick, her bald head stylishly swathed, and just ordinarily preoccupied by the arrival in an unfamiliar country.

Andy and I had not been there long and did not know many people yet. I had an Amah, Ah Wah, sent straight from heaven. She looked after our family's every need. I had nowhere to go and no one to see. Maggie and I had ten days to spend together, talking, laughing, crying and most importantly being honest. I was still thinking major, unbelievable, turn around miracles. She stopped me in my tracks. "Jo, I am going to die. If you can't accept that I have wasted my time coming to see you." Clear, concise and to the point. I stopped pretending. She had opened the door to a different perspective: we had the miracle of being able to share thoughts of death, loss and ideas of what might be beyond.

Then my children would pile in, and we would be playing Animal Lotto with laughter and joy. Her two year old Godson, Tom, heart wrenchingly offered to lend her one of his legs. There is video film somewhere of the children all hopping to see what it would be like to have only one leg. We hired a beach house in

Srini   Jo & Oliver   Maggie & Pete   Thomas   Andy

Port Dickson and Andy and Srini carried Maggie into the sea, which was as hot as a bath. She hadn't thought she would ever swim again, and this was unimagined luxury.

We did get another miracle in Kuala Lumpur. Palliative care in 1982 was in its infancy and Maggie was rarely out of pain but for all the time they were with us, she remained pain-free. This underlining of the pain-free days she had experienced at the time of the ticket booking was another thing to be grateful for. The parting was agony. We both knew we were seeing each other for the last time - although neither of us was enlightened or brave enough to admit it. Maggie went with Srini in this weakened state to meet with her in-laws in India. How strange it must

Maggie's final entry into the visitors book Feb 15 1982

4

have been for all of them?

I only appreciated the enormity of the gift that she had given me in retrospect. Even her closest friend never had 10 minutes with her, let alone 10 days. Andy and I keep a visitors' book. When I was checking exact dates I realized the idea to create this book came 25 years to the day of Maggie arriving in Kuala Lumpur. Another miracle? A coincidence? My own deep memory nudging me? I don't know, but I do know that yet again I am reassured that this story has to be told - and that this is the time.

Maggie in her own Words.

London, Ontario, Canada

30th April 1982

I'm sitting on the floor of our bedroom in 444

Belvedere Avenue in London,

and I am just wondering where

you are, sitting listening to

this, or how old you are.

I am going to try and record a

few things to you.

I thought of writing them down, I tried writing them

down, preparing it a little, but I think the best way will

be just to speak to you now and again until the tape is

finished.

Today is May.....no, it's not quite .

Today is the 30th of April, 1982.

It is a beautiful evening outside. It is about 7 o'clock and Daddy has just gone to collect some piece of furniture, or get it changed. You are across the road with Matthew and Megan, in 445 Belvedere Avenue and I hope you are having your supper there and I won't have to give it to you here.

Jo's thoughts:

Maggie lays down her introduction in this simple way. Sitting on the floor as she loved to do, in her home in London, Ontario, and just speaking a gentle commentary on what is happening in the outside of her world. She notices the beauty of the day and anticipates the joy of seeing Francis and Srini again. It isn't hard to imagine what thoughts were running along inside her head, as she prepared to speak to her son across the years.

May 1st:

Now it is May 1st and I am in the house on my own,

waiting for you, ... you and your father to come home.

Srini did buy a bed last night, an enormous bed,

which I'm sure you still have in the house. It's a lovely

one, but you had to go back to the shop 3 times, right

across London, before he got the right parts for

it. He was none too pleased, and neither were you,

because you were waiting for your french fries to turn

up and things were being horribly delayed.

Jo's thoughts:

This little scene seems matter of fact but anyone who knew
Maggie and Srini would recognise the underlying determination
of Srini to get the new bed right. Maggie was probably thinking
"Oh for heaven's sake let it be" but Srini would not be diverted
from his purpose. That bed has huge significance, because it
represented for Srini the vitally important spark that was their
marriage. His strength as a husband to Maggie when everything
was gone, bar the complete and unconditional love that we all

promise our partners on our wedding day. He really meant those promises and lived up to them, providing an inspiration to all who believe in "till death us do part".

Francis Dear,

What should I tell you, that you might want to know

about me, or my life with your father,

and before your father?

Let me start with my own early days and then maybe I'll

talk about your early days

of which I've only seen a very few.

I was born, as I'm sure you know, in Glasgow in Scotland

and I was number...... fifth in a family of seven.

Jo's thoughts:
I was fourth and her big sister. Two and a half years separated us. We shared the same bedroom and hours and hours of chatter, games, and secrets.

There were eight originally but one died early, after birth.

We lived in a fairly large house in Glasgow.

Jo's thoughts:

We moved from a small house in the grounds of Stobhill Hospital where my father was the assistant administrator, to a much larger house on the south side of Glasgow. My father had returned to clinical medicine, and took up a position as a geriatrician. I was seven and Maggie was five.

Both Nanie and Papa were doctors, as you know, and they struggled. Seven children, I don't think, was ever an easy thing. It was never an easy thing to make ends meet with seven children, but they managed very well. We were a happy bunch. We all used to go on holidays together and I would say we got on very well as a family, and we still do up until this day.

This is no exaggeration. This story can be told because of the love that we witnessed between our parents. Their love and respect for each other, and beyond, taught us something we would never learn from books.

I don't think there is one of us who wouldn't travel a long way to see the other if they were in trouble.

At the time of her death the family was spread across four continents, and we criss-crossed the globe to see, to talk, to love and to support each other. Indeed my brother Gerry , who was teaching in Zambia at the time, with only telegram and slow airmail contact, had made the tortuous trek from Africa to see her for a few days just after the amputation of her leg. Such a gesture meant the world to Maggie.

What else? I think I was a fairly quiet and shy child. Maybe, being fifth in line you didn't get a chance to get to say many things, so I probably just kept quiet a good deal of the time.

Mags   Mother (Nanie)   Srini

Jo's thoughts:

She was a quiet child and was prepared to trot along behind me. Of all the children she was most like our mother. Physically , the resemblance was remarkable, and photographs of them both in childhood are almost identical. In character, I think they were more like each other than either would admit. They were shy young women, but they both pushed through that shyness and didn't allow it to limit them. Maggie shook it off and came to appreciate her great gifts. Again, my parents can take huge credit, as they were able to support and encourage this mix of introverts and extroverts that they had produced. An aspect of Mags' gentler side, that served her well, was her innate ability to listen to and attend to others. It was what made her a great doctor and a sensitive loving friend. There was a huge circle of people who were heartbroken at her death; people that we never knew but whose letters told the story.

13

I was reasonably industrious at school. I did quite well without trying too hard.

And, I took music lessons, violin lessons, as you will see by the violin that's left for you.

We all did, we all took violin and piano lessons. Some fell by the wayside. In fact most fell by the wayside, we didn't really make much of it but we learned anyway.

Jo's thoughts:
Maggie was incredibly musical and loved to sing, dance and to play her violin. She sang and toured with the Scottish National Chorus but could also stand up and sing jazz. Indeed she did this with the band on her own wedding day.

And then school.

I think school for me was a pretty uneventful kind of time, and I don't remember too much about it. It certainly wasn't unhappy, but I don't remember it with any terrific enthusiasm.

Jo's thoughts:
I love the casual way she dismisses her school career. Maggie was probably the most gifted academically of all of us and won prize after prize on a regular basis. She was always around the top of the class, and was conscientious to a degree that was alien to me. She never failed an exam, nor ever got into any kind of trouble, whereas I bounced along cheerfully in bottom sets for everything. She never gave up on her violin and derived immense pleasure from it. This is surely a huge lesson to all of us who stress over our children's education. Perhaps they won't even remember it!

I left school when I was sixteen and I went straight into Glasgow University then, to do medicine. And that was a fine time. I enjoyed that. Again, I stayed at home

then......It was a rigorous kind of course. You had to

work fairly hard. I was young and not too confident, so

I probably overdid it, and and didn't enjoy university

life to the full, but perhaps many people say that.

Maybe if I had my time again I wouldn't do it any

different. However I finished university and I felt

then definitely that I was going to spread my wings,

and I looked around for a job outside Glasgow.

And I found one as a house surgeon in Leicester in

England, and that's where I met your dad.

Jo's thoughts:

She did leave home at this stage and she began to flower in her
independence. She embraced the new life with enthusiasm, joined
clubs, took up hockey, continued with her singing and playing.
I have to admit that this time of her life is a bit of a blank for me
as we went our separate ways. I know that she and I were falling

in and out of love with assorted folk. I was in Berlin and she was in Leicester. We phoned from time to time and met up at home fleetingly. Suddenly, one day she turned up in Berlin, with a wild Afro hairdo. I hardly recognised her. Andy and I had decided to get engaged and she was happy as I had ever seen her with her new man - Srini. Although there was much sadness, stress, tears and misunderstandings before they were finally married, I knew in that short week-end that we spent with them in Berlin, that she was utterly at peace in his company. Somehow their spirits knew what many people from both families took a long time to accept.

How am I doing so far?

I seem to have reached the age of 23 without telling you very much. Would you be interested in maybe what kind of things we did when we were kids? We used to go amazing holidays. Papa, my father, was the best organiser in the world.

Jo's thoughts:

This is an abiding memory for all of us. My father married late in life and I think he realised that the only route to survival was military style organisation. He was a very gentle leader though.

He used to be packing the car, preparing to pack the car, weeks ahead of the holiday. I would say, almost in direct contrast to Srini, your own father, who would be packing (he would get it all done mind you) the night before. Shove it in!

Jo's thoughts:

True again, the better we got to know Srini it was a constant surprise to witness his style, but he did always get things done.

But Papa was meticulous. Everything had to be right.

And when you think about it, to get nine people going on holiday in a V.W. Beetle, you had to do a bit of thinking. And that's what we did. We used to go on holiday in a Beetle. I don't even know if they are still around .I don't think they make them anymore, certainly not in Germany. But we did.

There was two in the back cubby hole, four in the back seat, and my Mother and Father and the baby Bernard in the front. (she sniffs) Excuse me. And the whole car would be packed up to the hilt. We were allowed one small plastic bag with our clothes in and that was it. No extras. But it was great fun. We had some.....we had some fantastic holidays. We used to go to St Andrews in Scotland, we used to go to Girvan and we used to go to Ireland.

Jo's thoughts:

This part sounds fanciful, but it is true that we all went on holiday in this little car. She and I were the "two in the cubby hole". I think V.W. may have called it a boot but it was covered in a kind of rough carpet and we sat knee to knee clutching our plastic bags and chatting, free from the pestering of our brothers. Other cars were introduced and everyone's favourite was a V.W. caravanette, in which we slept everyone except the "big boys" who were banished to some funny old tent because they were supposed to be scouts, which was a joke as they didn't have a clue about scouting. The family camping holidays are the stuff of myth and legend. Choosing the headland at Ballybunion in southern Ireland was crazy. One night the wind took away our latrine tent and brought down the rest of the equipment. We were rescued by the local priest and we spent the rest of the time in a church hall. I don't know what my mother thought of all this but it must have been the most unspeakable hassle for her. My father loved it as he had his little troop to organise and influence, and instil his philosophy of life without the distraction of school and the outside world.

I don't think we ever went, no, we never went abroad as a family, we just used to........., it was just too much and probably too expensive. Anyway we enjoyed that kind of thing. We had great, a lot of good times as a family. We used to have..... the birthdays....the birthdays were an exercise. Everyone at the birthday had to make a speech about the person whose birthday it was. So you would go round the whole family saying what do you think about this person.

Well we used to be fairly.......I was shy at them all, all I used to say was "Happy Birthday, I hope you have a nice time." But the boys, Johnny and Frank, Bernard and Gerard were so...., as the years went by they got funnier and funnier.

Jo's thoughts:

I know Maggie would have said more about the birthdays if Frances and Srini hadn't arrived home. The birthdays in our house were absolutely integral and central to our family life. To miss one was unthinkable, although in later years we moved the celebration to a day when everyone could be present. We didn't often have other children in to celebrate our birthdays, but from the moment you woke up, you were the "birthday person". Other family members would pile into the bedroom and waken you up with singing. You felt special all day long. The real deal though was at the evening meal which would be your choice. We all had our own places at the table but on birthdays the birthday person, moved and sat beside my father. After the meal was served the highlight came - the presents and the speeches. A master of ceremonies would be appointed, and the speeches and presentation would go in the order chosen by the M.C. except for the last three speeches. When all the other children had finished speaking, competing with anecdotes either kindly or funny, my mother would recall the actual birth day of the child and remind us of the joy she had felt at the arrival, and then my father would talk about the child but also about the importance of family life and what joy we all brought to our parents. Then the birthday person spoke a thank you to everyone. Initially as she says this was a daunting business but we all came to love those birthdays. At least one day a year you got this wonderful injection of positive encouragement and unconditional love. The unit was sealed again and again and my wonderful parents were laying down the foundations, layer upon layer of the love that sustained us, nourished us and led us to the attitudes that Maggie was able to express in this message to her child. The most famous birthday in the family history is probably my ninth birthday because it was cancelled due to my bad behaviour. No point in hiding it now. I mooned to my classmates and got caught. Can you imagine what the nuns thought of that in 1955? My parents were asked to impose a punishment that I would remember! I do and so do all of us. I can still bring tears of regret to my aged mother if I am feeling unkind! No cards, no presents, no speeches and no singing. What a day!

Oh I think, yes you're home, so is Daddy. I can hear you coming in the back door.

O.K. I will just pause just now

Mags: Francis

Francis: Yep

Mags: Are you coming? Would you like to hear yourself on the tape? Hello, hello,   Francis what have you been doing?

the tape's on, the tape's on . Say hello to yourself.

Francis: Eh

Mags: Hello Francis, say hello Francis!

Srini: Hi Francis

Jo's thoughts:
Mgt and Srini try to get Francis to talk into the tape. An ordinary little family exchange.

May 8th: Recorded in Hospital

Francis , the date is now May the 8th. And over the last few days my health has gone down again and I have had to come into hospital. I have lost the power in my legs, my right leg, and probably from the waist down. I can't move very well. I didn't intend or plan to talk to you too much about this cancer that I've had and that Srini and I have had to deal with for the last two years. More or less since you've been born. But here I am in this situation where it has suddenly hit me and Srini again and you now. Once again, we don't really know exactly what is going to happen, or when. So I am just going to talk to you whenever I feel like it, whenever I can, and try to give you some idea of what it all means to us.

You, Francis, since you've been born, have never given us any cause but for great joy, apart from a few odd nights when you wouldn't go to sleep. You have been......well...you've just been part of us since we've been together and married. We knew you were coming about three months after we were married, and immediately you were part of our lives and as so you are now, and such a joyous part and happy part of our lives.

How does a mother explain to you what a wonderful joy it is to have you around?

I'll pause there for a moment Francis.

Jo's thoughts:

At this precise time Maggie and I were exchanging letters. I in Kuala Lumpur was in an agony of not knowing how she was feeling. But re reading the letters of the time shows how much she was still thinking of all of us although she was sharing her story with her child. At this time I found a poem about the joy of having a sister. I sent it to her and she tells me that it allowed much needed tears to flow as she was rapidly losing her physical power.

May 10th: (letter from Jo to her sister, Maggie)

Kuala Lumpur

May 10th 1982

Dearest Maggie

Here is the poem I promised to send you. I can't claim to have written it, but by God I could have because it says everything I would ever try to say.

If it makes you cry - well fine because it made me cry buckets and buckets.

I loved our phone call it was solid gold (in more ways than one!!) So good, so very good to talk to you and for you to say you feel me near you, because I am dearest Maggie, every single minute of the day and I'm only sad sometimes which is fine.

Like you said on the phone, thank goodness it was your bottom half and not top half that went so you can enjoy all your visitors – how I'd love to have been one of them.

"We will merrily meet" elsewhere.

We moved my birthday to Sunday as it was more convenient all round and I had a beautiful day. My men folk spoiled me totally all day long and Andy sprung a surprise tea party in the afternoon with some friends "dropping in". Ah Wah made

the most stupendous cake and so we had a lovely time.
My two days teaching went off OK last week and I must say it
was nice to be in front of some "big kids" for a change.
I'm involved up to my neck in the "Wives Club" cultural show
which is an annual presentation.

The Scottish dancing is a very big item and I'm going
crazy trying to get my "gels" to dance in a circle. I'm also
the bridegroom in a portrayal of a Malay wedding and I'm
finding my words a bit hard to learn.

Andy and les garcons are fantastically well and all give me
tremendous joy. Andy and I are seven years married this
month, can you believe it? And I believe, going from strength
to strength, which is lovely – (three steps forward and only one
step back!!)

Yes the Falklands crisis is no longer a laughing matter and I
sincerely hope that the U.N. can sort something out.
Well I'll sign off now and look forward to your letters.
I love and miss you always my dearest darling Maggie.

All love Jo
xxx

<u>Psalm for a Sister</u>   (anon..)

I will lift up my eyes and smile
As I give thanks for my sister.
My radiant complicated sister,
Who is more than a sister,
Who is my friend.
(Blessed be the woman who has one like her and thrice blessed if she has
more than one.)
I will thank the good Lord that we were children together,
Sharing the same room for years.
I rejoice to remember our games and plans.
Our secrets and surprises-even our quarrels.
I feel a deep, poignant longing for those days when we were girls together.
Life hungry-love hungry,
Each fighting her own battle yet supporting the other against the world.
My sister oh Lord my beautiful sister;
Often maddening, always understanding, always fun.
Thank you for this woman who shares my parents,
My past, my blood;
Who sees me whole-the beginning-the long ago and the person that I am now.
My sister whose faults are so clear to me and dear to me, as mine are to her.
Yet for all our differences and the miles that lie between,
We would still battle the world for each other.
I laugh for the joy of my sister, all the comedy and gaiety,
And I sometimes weep for my sister.
I long to comfort her,
To hold her close, as we held each other for comfort or courage
 when we were little girls.
Dear God please take very good care of this sister that I love so much.

May: Recorded in hospital a few days later

Anybody listening to our story of our life over the last few years, may think how sad, what a sad tale it all is, that a young family, very happy, should lose one of its members fairly early on in life. And we've seen it that way too. ......how sad it is, we possibly can't spend much more time together.

Jo's thoughts:
What I love about this poignant part of the tape is her absolute honesty. She is facing up to her situation, was accepting of it and striving to understand it. She never asks "Why?" There was no "victim" in her thinking, just an understanding that LIFE happens and what you do with it is the thing that forms you.

Well, Francis I can only say, that there's been so many moments of sheer joy in the time that I have spent with your father, and in the time that we've spent together with you. I don't know or I can't think that many people could have had more happy moments than we have had. I am sure in the years to come, Francis, you and your daddy will have clashes, disagreements, arguments, but the love and the bond that I see between you both now, will never be lost. It really is an impossible task to say in words the meaning of the life, albeit short, that I have had with Srini. He is the most wonderful man to be loved by and to love. And I simply thank God that I have had

the opportunity in my life to be in this position, of giving and receiving such a love.

Srini   Mags

Francis,

Perhaps this is not a bad time to mention, or speak about a few things that are close to my heart. In the way of God, Christ, religion. I certainly believe in God's hand having an effect in life. I can't say I understand the meaning of all the things that happen, why they happen, why they should happen to us. But in all this time, I have never felt bitter, or why should this have happened to me. I feel more, why not? It's happened to others, it's part of life, of living, and it's more important how these things affect you rather than why did they affect you. The most concrete evidence, or surely not evidence, but the most strongest feeling I have had during all this time is one of the tremendous power and influence of the Good Lord in everything. The fact that I can be here talking to you on the tape, this is wonderful. The kind of support, and love, and encouragement we've had as a family, from my family, from Srini's family is immeasurable. And the wonderful feelings and emotions which this has inspired in us is again something, which I think, perhaps, not many people experience in their lives.

May 19th : letter from Maggie to Jo

Hopefully by tomorrow – this is my last night in hospital

May 19th 1982

Dearest darling Jo

Two letters arrived today from you, one general one and one for me. I don't believe you didn't write it or if you didn't, you certainly could have.

For the first time since I came in here I cried well and it was a wonderful feeling. I needed it and you were able to trigger it off for me. But I could send the psalm to you and with exactly the same sentiment, how close it came to describing us, not close, but that was and is our relationship - what a joy to know it and feel it and express it.

Since coming back to London, I had been feeling kind of dry of enthusiasm and a bit lost but recently again I find hope and a lot of joy has crept back in and it is a relief. Srini also is relaxing and we are talking together again without picking holes in what each other is saying.

I'm thrilled about getting home and ready to make a go of it. Mary is loving planning to get up for my two hourly injections or "feeds" of medicine and Mother is relaxing nicely and pandering to me, and I love it.

I'll be able to tell you more of the goings on once I get settled in "444" again.

Sorry about the telegram! I forgot about them arriving at all hours of the day and night. However, I was delighted to hear about the surprise party and Ah wah's cake – it's so good to be able to picture the scene exactly as it must have been with the four lads creating the birthday atmosphere and then having some surprise guests.

Hope you finally got card and letter, thought they wouldn't arrive in time, hence telegram!

And of course it's your seventh anniversary. I'm sure I told you about my seven year theory in marriage – it always seems to me that around seven years couples who are really couples seem to suddenly kind of blossom – I felt that when we came to see you in Kuala Lumpur. I could feel your togetherness; it had a kind of solidity and unshakeableness to it. Terrible description but it says what I mean. I don't think we have quite reached it yet but have no doubts that it's coming. Happy anniversary always - wonderful memories around the time of your wedding.

More very soon from all of us here. You know you are always with us.

Your ever-loving sister
Mags

p.s. You know how all the letters get passed round everybody but I've kept my letter and "psalm" to myself, between us – I just felt like that, I want to treasure it.

May 20th : Bernard's Letter written while he was visiting London

Bernard Dunn

444 Belvedere Avenue

London

Ontario

20 May 1982

Dearest Jo & Andy & Boys,

It is about 11pm here, and Srini and I are the only ones left up. Maggie came home about 5.30 this evening and I cannot say how happy we all are that this happened. It was always her wish that she should come home, and now that we are all together all the time during this period, it makes these precious days even more special. I arrived here in Toronto last Friday about 7pm and after a really rough time from customs. Frank was waiting as I passed out of the gate. It was important and revealing for me to have the chat with Frank during the 2-hour journey to London. He had been here during the whole of the previous week with Mags and Srini, while Mags had gone through both good and bad times, so he was able to make the situation pretty clear to me that Mags did not have long until she was to be with God, and that these evil tumours were widespread. When I met Mags at the hospital, it was wonderful even though I had seen her only two months previously. After a very short period you just felt that you were not talking to someone very close to death. Maggie was so alert, serene, calm and straight talking. As you know Mum decided to go out to Canada 4 days before me when Mags became pretty ill.

My great worry was that Maggie might die before I arrived on Friday the 14th. Even though words have all been said, the lovely thing is to be with Mags, and chat about everything and to just be around. The visits to the hospital have been so happy and peaceful and the overriding feeling for me is that Mags is going to be with me and us all for many, many years after she leaves us down here. I honestly feel that she is going to guide us in things that we do in the future.

We got your 2 letters yesterday morning – one to Mags – one to everyone else. Great as usual.

We have a good wee routine here. We get up about 8.30 and have tea, toast and orange juice. Then do some shopping in town, and then to the hospital about 12.00. Stay for about an hour then go for some lunch. Return about 2 o'clock and stay with Mags for the rest of the afternoon. We have talked about everything from family holidays to the Falklands crisis.

Another feeling that I am even more certain of, having been here almost one week, is that all of us are playing just as important a role of support, no matter where they are, and that means all of you. It seems like ages and much water under the bridges since you left on November 30th last year. It will be a wonderful reunion, when we are all together again perhaps for Mum and Dad's 40th anniversary next year, although the sadness of Maggie will be with us. I am trying to play the role of general skivvy and support giver here just now. I am due to return home on Saturday 29th May and I think that no matter what happens I go home then.

Daddy needs a lot of support and it must be lonely for him at home. But I convinced him that another trip out here would be a bit much.

I will close now as time goes on. Mother and Mary are both well and fine weather makes us all feel a bit better. I miss you all very, very much.

With much love.
Bernard

May 23rd: Home from Hospital

Darling Francis,

I have moved onto a new day. It's almost the end of
May. May 23rd I think it is. I am home from hospital,
and such a joy it is to be home too. Oh! You would
be surprised at the organization in this room where
I am lying, in my bed, talking to you. Mary, your
Aunt Mary, your godmother, is here and Nanie and
Bernard. Just helping out, looking after me. I suppose
the biggest difference for me now, since going into
hospital this time, is I can no longer get myself from A
to B, so I have to be carried. And that's probably the
only difference, and it doesn't bother me too much and
it doesn't seem to bother anybody else. So I usually
spend most of my time in the room here in the morning,

then get up and go into the front room and stay there for some time. And that's more or less the order of the day, sounds boring doesn't it. Well it's not.

Jo's thoughts:
Mary's Role

Mary, my elder sister, was a fabulous nurse. She was also a person of immense empathy and courage. She lived in Dublin and was very busy with four young children. Like the rest of us she was in constant touch with Canada but was unable to be there because of all her commitments.

When it became obvious that Maggie's time on earth was short and specialised nursing was the only way she could stay at home, Mary decided it was time for the big guns. She did not want anyone else taking her wee sister on her last journey. Mary organised her family and went to Canada for an extended time and made it possible for Maggie to stay at home until she died. She established a regime of care that was second to none.

The family were taking turns to visit and to contribute as best they could to Maggie's last weeks. Our family is laden with doctors and my parents found it hard to be just parents and not to interfere with the medical regime especially when Srini took decisions which they didn't quite understand. They seemed to age furiously at this time.

Mary was a business like and authoritative figure of immense tenderness. Maggie gives no details of what those days were like but Mary told me that the "getting up "was the most tortuous and excruciating process. At every stage she apologised to Mags for the pain she had to inflict. My brothers' letters describe how Mary was only ever sleeping for two hours a day so that she would be available for Maggie's drugs and injections.

At this time palliative care tended to be reactive rather than proactive. Pain relief was not sophisticated and Maggie's pain was hard to control. Maggie gives no hint of this in the tape. Her total acceptance of the steady march of the illness is still hard to credit but I notice how often she uses the word "joy" to describe her experience.

O.K. Francis.

Let's see if I can tell you what you are up to these days. Even in two short weeks, I come home and you are talking more. Asking "What?" "Why?" after every sentence. Running around. Still won't go to bed at night ......but we don't mind. What else do you do?

There's a boy across the road, Matthew of course,

your buddy; most of the day you spend your time

trying to get over to see Matthew and Megan, which

you do successfully.

You certainly have a mind

of your own these days,

and I suppose that's just

about right.

comes into the room and there is a heart warming session as she tries to get Francis to sing "Doh A Deer" from 'The Sound of Music'. So the last we hear of her is her very pure voice singing even in her extremely weakened state. Their little singing session was halted by my sister Mary coming into the room to say that our mother was on the phone.

There is such joy in this section of the tape even though it is the end. She was so close to death and yet the voice is still full of fun and clarity. Even the way she encourages Francis to join her is a simple example of perfect parenting. Maggie's health deteriorated significantly after this and she was never able to continue with the tape. She died on June 27th with only her beloved Srini at her side.

June 29th:

letter from Dr Frank (Francis) Dunn to his brothers
and sisters after Maggie's death

444 Belvedere Ave

London

29th June 1982

Dearest Mary, David and family.

Dearest John, Carol and boys

Dearest Jo, Andy and family.

Dearest Gerry and Marion

Dearest Bernard.

I am very aware of sadness experienced by yourselves over the
past few days and the frustration of not being together at this
time. We have also experienced sadness at Maggie's death, but
somehow I feel it was more difficult for those not in London
physically, and therefore, as promised, I am sending you a full
account of the events of the last week.

Maggie's death is also the start of a new life for her and we are
relieved that she is free of sufferings. Why then do we experience
great waves of sadness? For me it is the loss of a dear friend and
sister and it leaves a big hole. People will eventually say "you'll
get over it" but I don't want to get over it. I'll certainly, in time,
adapt to Maggie's departure from this life but things will never
be quite the same. I'll strive to learn from her life in order to
improve my own. As I said to her a few weeks ago, "we'll continue

to communicate" and she also felt that would be the case.

I arrived in London at the bus station to be met by Anne Marie, a friend of Maggie's. She said that Maggie had suffered a major deterioration that afternoon and Mum and Dad could not leave. She assured me that Mags was still alive. When we got to the house I went straight to Maggie's bedroom to find her very distressed, and having breathing difficulties. That day she had lost her ability both to cough and to swallow and an I.V. had been started. She was aware of my presence but I thought slightly delirious. In general the change from May when I last saw her was very marked and frankly I felt she would die that evening. Despite her critical condition, she actually managed to hum a few songs with Mother and Dad. Her breathing continued to be laboured that night, although later she became lucid and we exchanged a few words. She asked for Helen and "the wee man" as she always called Andrew. She said my name a few times, but was too weak to carry on any conversation. That night in the den we could hear her laboured breathing and I know Mother slept little, if at all, that night.

On Tuesday a.m. her breathing pattern had improved and she was slightly more responsive. Srini taped the Messiah and this allowed us to play it on her machine. As they sang "Comfort Ye", the emotions were running very high. Srini then played the S.N.O. (Scottish National Orchestra) choir singing Scottish songs and Mags enjoyed that. The loss of swallowing meant of course that the morphine had to be given by injection. Fortunately

Maggie did not feel the injections because of the loss of sensation below the waist. Mother was on top form and relaxed with her role as daytime nurse. (Incidentally, everyone was full of praise for the way Mary had set up the whole nursing programme). The remainder of Tuesday passed fairly uneventfully.

Mother discovered that Maggie found ice lollies very soothing though even fluids were difficult to swallow. Monsignor Roney administered Holy Communion a particle of which Maggie managed to swallow. Tuesday night was fairly uneventful except for progressing weakness.

Early Wednesday Mags looked very weak and could not communicate. Inge arrived to see her and suddenly she opened her eyes and they embraced. It was a poignant moment and they conversed. (Mags predominantly with her eyes.) Mags also had some great banter with Srini, she kept dropping her ice lolly and Srini moved to take it off her but Mags wouldn't let him. She then dropped it again and said, "I'm a bit of a fraud". Incidentally, when Mother took the lollipop away the day before Mags said, "You're an old meanie". Wednesday afternoon, evening and night were times of almost total sleep without obvious pain. The question of alternative methods of feeding were discussed but in general it was felt that their interventions would not save Maggie's suffering and in any event, she was too weak. Maggie received Communion for the last time.

Thursday saw a further deterioration in Maggie's conscious level and from then on we were unable to communicate with her.

Around 11pm she developed serious breathing difficulties with associated severe distress. Her agitation did not respond to the usual treatment and therefore Srini and I went to the hospital for further supplies. Her condition stabilised by 1am and remained with her for most of that night. It was so frustrating to see her lying there and not be able to converse. Mags just loved to chat and life without communication, she could not have accepted. We were all surprised she survived that night.

On Friday she was marginally better though still unconscious. On Saturday her breathing was definitely more relaxed and she had a beautiful, peaceful day. Mother and Dad went to evening Mass and Srini and I stayed with Mags. Srini was very sad on Saturday and although we felt happier that day, I'm sure subconsciously he felt the end was very near. Saturday night was very peaceful for her.

We always went to 11am Mass on a Sunday on all my previous visits here but this time we decided to go to 9.30 Mass. Srini wanted to stay with Mags. Francis came and Mother and Dad decided to also come. It was a very quiet Mass finishing at 10.40am. For some unknown reason we decided to take Francis across to Springbank Park for a shot on the swings. We then went for a paper and back to 444. As we came towards the front door I heard the Messiah on the record player in the front room, which struck me as very strange and ominous since Maggie had her own tape machine and Srini had recorded the Messiah for her previously. I know this all sounds superfluous, but it struck me so forcibly at the time. I went ahead of Mother and Dad and Srini appeared crying at the front door. "It's all over," he said to me. I gave him a hug and told Mother and Dad. We all wept and went in to see her. She was very peaceful and at rest. In actual fact it was very apt that Srini should have that last private moment with Mags. Despite the fact that we knew her death was imminent, it came as a bit of a jolt and somehow the general feeling was that it was as unreal as her illness had been real. We prayed for some minutes at her bedside. Everyone was very calm especially Mother. (I suspect that it would have been a bit harder for her if she had been present at the moment of death.)

July 1st (Frank continues his letter)

As always happens in such situations, there was no time for morose contemplation and we all set about organising the funeral. Mother and Srini undertook the initial preparations in Mags' room. I contacted the undertaker and made the necessary calls and Dad tidied up generally and actually hoovered the whole house. In the afternoon Srini and I went to the Funeral Home to complete the arrangements. It was very quick and easy, as Mags had already arranged everything down to the last detail. I thought this was a remarkable act of love for Srini, taking the strain of decision- making, i.e. coffin etc off him. Mags' body came back to the house that evening and to the bedroom on the right at the end of the hall where she had spent the last few weeks. The room looked lovely, bedecked with flowers and with a stunning picture of Mags taken some years ago by Srini in Scotland. She looked good in that – windswept, happy and relaxed.

In Loving Remembrance
of
MARGARET CHARY
(nee Dunn)
who died in Canada
27th JUNE, 1982
Aged 31 years.
Fortified by the Rites of Holy Church

Eternal rest grant unto her, O Lord, and let perpetual light shine upon her. May she rest in peace. — Amen.

Srini had got this enlarged and uplifted on Friday. We, like you Jo, felt that it was not Mags but her temple that had returned to the house. It was very evident that she was in a better place. Nonetheless it was a great comfort to those who had not seen her for some time to see her at peace. It was also a lovely environment for us to pray and to reflect on her life and her sufferings. May she rest in peace.

The next two days flew in – visitors to the house, preparation for the day of the funeral, choosing readings phone calls etc etc. On Monday night we had prayers at the house and unlike the UK, the body remains at home overnight. The day of the funeral was of course Tuesday and the pall bearers arrived at 10.30am at the house. They were Hayden Bush, Peter Boyle, Jim Telford (Inge's husband), Dr Webster and Dr Gilchrist and me. The church was well filled. I did the first readings (Wisdom 3. 1-9) and with God's and

Maggie's help, remained in reasonable control. I also read out the bidding prayers, which were greatly appreciated by all. Monsignor Roney, who as you know does not mince his words and is very candid, paid unstinting praise to Mags. He said that he had never in all his years of assisting the dying seen someone so able to come to terms with death. He also fittingly paid tribute to Srini's devotion and loving support to Mags. The cremation followed later that day and tomorrow Mags' ashes will be interred at St Peter's Cemetery.

We returned to 444 after the service and about thirty people joined us in an alfresco lunch in the back garden. The whole meal was laid on by volunteers from the parish and from the Cancer Clinic. Certainly not a morose occasion. By 2.30pm it was all over. The last three days have been spent relaxing, talking and helping Srini. He has kept busy returning items to the hospital and re-arranging rooms. Mother has been sorting out some personal things of Mags' and we have been discussing with Srini his immediate plans. Again, fortunately, Mags and Srini had discussed this. A high priority is for Srini to pass his exam and he will therefore take this in September. Francis will return with Mother and Dad to Glasgow on July 8th and Srini will visit them at the end of September.

Srini had handled himself magnificently throughout the last three years and we could not hope for a better brother in law and have wished for a better husband for Maggie during this time. He told me today how already he misses coming home to tell Mags the small things that happened during the day. We must pray that God will help him get through the early, most difficult times and however sad we may feel, his loss is the most profound.

I don't need to sing Mother and Daddy's praises here. We all know what they've been through and their commitment to Mags over this time reflects their love for all of us. I can assure you all that they supported me as much and more than I supported them.

I can think of no better way to end than with two quotations from the Requiem Mass (Wisdom 3).

> "In the eyes of the unwise they did appear to die,
> their going looked like a disaster,
> their leaving us like annihilation
> but they are in peace".

> "God has put them to the test and proved them worthy to be with him".

May she rest in peace.

Your loving brother
Francis. (Frank)

July 9th:

Eldest brother Johnny's letter written a few weeks after Maggie's death

Glasgow

9.7.82

Dear Jo & Andy & Boys

Thank you for your letter of 28/6, which we found most moving as it released our emotional 'valves' a bit. We too have been a bit 'dry' and accepting since dear Mags passed on. I think this was due to the fact that I had seen the reality, knew what was inevitable and conveyed this to Carol. We really had a good cry the night we received your letter.

The sense of loss I feel is sometimes overwhelming, as she was such a warm, loving person, as well as the wonderfully forthright personality, which was with her right to the end. The thought of 'never' is very hard to accept. It will have to be as a 'glorified being'. I think that Mags as a 'glorified being' should be something rather wonderful.

It is worthwhile, I think, to start from Friday 4th June. Uneventful flight from Prestwick to Toronto, and on to London, Ontario. Taxi to '444'. Mary and a nurse were giving Mags a bed bath, so I couldn't see her right away. Then I went in after a little while. It was a lovely meeting, but I couldn't give her the hug I wanted, as she was so sore. She said 'Take it easy now'. Mary had done an incredible job in the three weeks she was there, and was leaving two days after my arrival. She was normally up day and night tending to Mags, as she, at this stage, could do nothing for herself. Mary had only 2 hours sleep every night. She has incredible stamina; she kept encouraging Mags to make the big efforts to get through all these awful things she had to do, enemas, catheter changing and all the drugs, pain and loss of dignity.

The next day I had a great chat with Mags. The chats had to be taken easily, nothing too heavy, just stop if she felt a bit tired. I would just look at her, and when she woke she would just smile. These were sad but wonderful moments. She asked all about my problems, and understood them and said I must battle on. We talked of people, music and other things. Mags never got round to recording all these classical pieces for Francis so she asked me if I would do that, so during the day I did this, till a large selection was built up. She was very happy this was done.

She told me also that she was at the end of her tether, and did not want to go through any more. 'Why does He want me to go through more'. She really had no desire to keep living. This feeling was real, and I went to bed that night, and prayed that the Dear Lord would not ask her for too much more. But she continued on, and was still able to make a joke and have lots of nice things to say to everyone.

You see, Jo and Andy, there was so much to cope with. Even the act of getting into the chair gave her a frightful and frightening expression, and shakes that really made me feel uneasy inside. Then there was the discomfort in her bowel area. So, on the Saturday afternoon of the day I arrived, there were people coming from Montreal to see her. She didn't get up; they came through to the room. She was feeling not too bad and then had a nosebleed. This was the tumour breaking through to the nose. It was stopped, but always, from then on, oozed a bit. There was also a large secondary in the roof of her mouth, that was affecting her swallowing.

On the Tuesday of my first week, in the morning, Srini was worried, as there had been a change. She was a bit confused and lapsing into semi-consciousness. Nurses and doctors thought that the time was maybe coming that I should get in touch with Mother and Dad. However, I was with her for an hour during that morning and just held her hand and cried buckets and she said 'Just let it all go.' I think she thought that this was maybe it, but no, she recovered in the evening and was a bit better in relative terms. M & D arrived by the Thursday, and I think it was providential that I told them to come out, because they had a week with Mags when she was quite clear and coherent, although there was an anxiety and depressive state escalating itself, which antidepressants had been given for. The high doses of morphine can induce this. Towards the end of my 2 weeks, this was being slightly better controlled, but things were pretty hard all round. On the second Saturday that I was there, Mags got up for her meal and asked to see her songbooks, and sang a few of her favourite ones. After that she decided that she would like to record, so I did that with her till 1.30 am! I have the recording, but have not played it yet. She sang 3 which was an incredible feat considering that she was so weak. The 'Magic' was still there. She sang 'Sunrise, Sunset', 'Send in the Clowns' and one other. I will arrange a copy for you. This was the only time, I am aware of, that she recorded. The parting the following week was very, very hard!

I got back home on Sunday 20th June and told Carol all that had happened. Back to work the next with so many thoughts. I phoned at 11.30 pm every night. On Tuesday 22nd, she was not able to take anything and was semi-conscious up to the end.

Mother has probably filled in the detail of the funeral so I will leave that.

We had our Mass late with over 100 relatives and friends. Fathers Willie and John, Father Gerard Dunn, Father John Mary and Father Terence were the 5 priests who concelebrated the Mass. Father Gerard gave a great homily, a great comfort, to us. Bernie and I read- I from WISDOM and Bernie from ROMANS. I read your bidding prayer. The Mass was in the front room, the altar near the window.

Mother and Dad arrived back on 11th July, 2 days ago (this letter has been interrupted) with Francis, as Srini is going for the exam again. So it's more work for them, but we will be helping. They are doing OK.

I am working very hard at the moment, but we are off on holiday on 1st August to St Andrews, to the house. We have it for the month. A much needed break.

I suppose Srini will stay put in London and get a nanny for Francis. This is the only way really, the practicalities of life dictate this; he really will have no option. He will feel so lonely at times I'm sure, but things will work out.

I will close now. We are thinking of you all. We are content with the knowledge our dearest Margaret is in heaven.

All our love as ever.

Johnny, Carol and the Boys.
XXXX

July 11th (approx)

Srini's words, ending as the tape runs out.
Spoken two weeks after Maggie's death.

O.K. Francis,

That's the last you'll hear of Mama now. I think its

been about two weeks since she has passed away and

I told you that she has gone to God. You saw Mama

and we went to the service. Monsignor Roney came

to the house to say the prayers. Mama was laid out

in the house for two nights, and lots of friends came

to see her. Nanie and Papa were here, so was Frank

at the service. After the service Mama was taken

away to the crematorium and we went to the chapel

there as well. It was one of the saddest days of my

life, that's life. I can't tell you how much I loved your

Mama, I know I'll miss her. I'll tell you more about her

anyway, in the future. This is just to let you know what I thought about her. She was the best friend I had. Maybe she will be around and talk to us, if not talk to us, just guide us in whatever we are doing. Nanie and Papa are going away to Glasgow and you will go to Glasgow with them. Then I will probably work for a few months and then bring you back home. My plan is to look after you. At least I see your Mama in you. O.K. I don't think nothing is going to happen to me, but if anything happens to me, I'm sure either Johnny and Carol or Josephine and Andy or Servotham and Salochanan , one of these three will look after you. Life is funny though. You really want some things in life and you go and search for them and you find them........(the tape ends)

July 24th:

Mary's letter to Jo, Andy and the boys a month after Maggie's death.

Laughonure

Co. Donegal

24th July 1982

My Dearest Jo, Andy and the boys.

It is four weeks today since Mags died and it is only now that I feel I can sit down and write to you. Does this seem strange? This does not mean to say I have not thought of you often – in fact more often that ever. It is just that I could not convey how I felt in a letter. There are so many things to tell you that it is hard to know where to begin.

The facts of what happened during the last few weeks you know already and so I will tell you now about my very special three weeks with Mags. First of all Jo, your little gift to me helped to pay my way and also I bought a very special bottle of champagne which we opened the night she came home – a most happy one. Mags was very touched that you had made this gesture and we felt that somehow you made that trip with me in spirit. She loved your letters too Jo and said to me that you always seemed to say the right thing at the right time.

However, to return to the story. Mags was worried about coming out of hospital after she lost all power from the ribcage down and she asked me several times on the phone if I was sure I could manage. You can imagine how determined I was to make the stay at home work out. In a combined effort between myself, Srini, Mother and the exceptional district nurses and Margaret, we worked out a very flexible routine and the days and nights ran as smoothly as possible. This was amazing when I think of what dear Mags suffered and that each day the ways of doing things to help her be a little more comfortable had to be changed e.g., we tried to find the best way of moving her without causing pain. One day you would think you had found the ideal way of moving without causing too much pain then following the same procedure the next day, she could not stand it. She was also taking so many different drugs that we had to waken her every two hours day and night to take them.

Every day she insisted on making the effort to get up and get dressed and then we carried her into the front room. She tried to take the main meal of the day with us but ate very little. This continued for about ten days and then Mother and Bernard went away home. Mags was getting weaker every day and then not able to get up so often. All through this her courage was amazing. Every hour brought its new challenge and ever hour she rose to meet it.

You can imagine how close we became during this time and how we talked about everything especially during the night. We had many laughs and a few cries, and I know too Jo, how close you and her were during all these years and I thought of you a lot during these days with her. I know you would have wanted to be there too but somehow <u>you were there</u>. It must have been all that love you were sending, I really believe in its power.

The last week of my stay was the most difficult. Mags was very tearful and felt very sad much of the time. She felt keenly that time was running out and she still had loads of things to do e.g. tapes for Francis, letters, cards etc. and she didn't have the energy to do them. She felt overwhelmed and afraid by the whole thing. I couldn't help but feel utterly helpless at these moments as I could plainly see that she had to travel this road alone. Usually she ended up reassuring me instead of the other way round! and inevitably we ended up laughing through the tears. Precious memories, Jo and Andy of a wonderful, courageous girl.

The time eventually came for me to leave and hand over to two new nurses. I found this very hard as I felt at this stage, probably arrogantly, that no-one could look after Mags like I could. I said goodbye to her knowing that this would be the last time but she said that this did not matter as we had said everything and anyway she would always be near us.

I told her I would ask God to give her peace of mind and a sense of feeling really near to him before she died, as she had felt so lonely during the last few days there. She said she would ask God for this too and she told me too that the few times that she had really asked for something he had never refused her. I made a novena to Our Lady of Perpetual Succour and she died on the ninth day, which also happened to be the feast of Our Lady of Perpetual Succour – an answer to prayer? - I hope so. The rest of the story you know already.

As you know, I also went to Scotland for one week. Mother and Dad gave us the usual welcome. They are great. They often feel sad but at the same time relieved to see Mags out of her suffering. I have wee Francis here with me in Ireland and thank God he has settled down really well and seems to be happy.

David has a great new job, he has been appointed chief executive of a chain of seventeen supermarkets here in Dublin. He loves the work and deserves it after all these years of little satisfaction.

Well dear Jo and Andy, I hope that this letter does not make you feel too sad but I am sure you want to know about my time with Mags.

With all my love. I hope things work out well with you both.

Mary xxx

About Mary

In the years that followed Maggie's death, Mary and I would recall this time often. She was happy to tell me and I was ever thirsty for the story. We were once travelling from Montrose to Glasgow and we were talking about Mags. Not in a morbid weepy way but just remembering her and somehow being with her, inviting her into our middleagedness. We got off the train in Glasgow and headed for the restaurant where we planned to have lunch. It was too busy so we chose somewhere else.

We sat down and were choosing our food when the song in the background was suddenly "I can't let Maggie go" by the Honeybus. Maggie loved this song as it was a favourite when she was a young teenager

"She flies like a bird in the sky....
She flies like a bird o me o my I see I sigh
Now I know I can't let Maggie go"
Somehow we felt she was with us.

As the years went by Mary and I became closer than we had been when younger. We never ever lived in the same country all through our adult lives. As the years went by and our children grew and our circumstances changed we embarked on an adult friendship which was a great joy. Then just when she was really happy, having come through a difficult divorce, Mary was diagnosed with cancer which was well advanced and terminal. I was then in a position to drop everything and be with her.

I got my chance to do for her what I had longed to do for Maggie. There was a triangular neatness about it which was just right. Mary had wonderful grown up children who accompanied her to her death with style, grace and maturity that would be an example for all. However I was just able to be a fellow traveller with her right up to the moment of departure. I thought of myself as wallpaper. Just there. No particular role except to be there. I thought about all the things that were on hold while I took this time out and then I realized this was not time out, it was time _in_ and real time in and probably the most important thing I would ever do. It was a real privilege. Somehow I feel as though this book has come into being because my sisters Mary and Maggie are together now.

July 28th:

letter from Inge in response to one from Jo (not available)

445 Belvedere Avenue

London, Ontario

28th July 1982

Dear Jo

Thank you so much for your lovely letter. Immediately after I read it, I began forming thoughts of what I'd like to write back to you, but I have so many things I'd like to say, I just don't know where to start. How I wish I could say them to you in person – you Jo, in particular because I know how close and how special you were to Margaret and it's hard to spill out all my emotions to someone who may not be feeling just the same way as I am.

As you say, there were many people who must have considered Margaret the best of friends. I must admit it took Margaret to convince me near the end that our feelings for each other were mutual. I guess I just respected and admired her so much, that I found it hard to believe that, with all her many friends, she considered me special as I did her. Her wonderful personality endeared her to so many people and her unique qualities touched everyone like magic. I could go on and on, but I don't think I need tell you about your own sister's character, though Margaret used to try to deny being as "good" as I would try to tell her she was.

I spent part of today sorting through some of her clothes that

Srini had brought over to me. I couldn't bring myself to do it before now. Srini said your mother had packed a box of things to be sent to Scotland. I hope I haven't been left with anything that you or anyone else may have wanted.

I can appreciate, Jo, how especially difficulty these last months must have been for you (not to mention the past three or four years) wanting to be with her and not being able to. I thought of you many times when I was able to spend some precious moments with her. I am very close to my sister too, and often found myself putting us in yours and Margaret's places. How frustrating it must have been for you. But as you said, it was good that you could be together last February and Margaret spoke of that visit with such joy. She's been so determined to get to you.

Part of my sadness is also that I have not lost one friend, but a whole family of wonderful people. I was fortunate enough to meet just about all of the Dunns and what a pleasure it was. When your mother and dad left, I felt as though a door were being closed that may never open again. That's why I was so thrilled when your letter came – to me it meant the door was not yet locked. I do hope you and your family will make that trip to Canada one day and that you will be in touch.

As you probably know, Srini is spending the weekdays at work in Toronto. The first weekend that he came home, I felt he seemed terribly lonesome, as can be expected, but true to his form, he was able to bear up and continue on as normally as possible – just as he did all through Margaret's illness, when

I'm sure he was suffering as much as she was. She couldn't have asked for a better partner to see her through the trauma.

Margaret has left us all with some beautiful memories that I for one will treasure forever. These days I don't think an hour goes by that I don't think of her. She expressed to me a long time ago how sad she thought it was that once a person had passed away, people speak of them less and less 'till finally their name is hardly even mentioned. She was referring to an old school friend's mother who had died whom all the girls thought so much of yet in time her name never came up anymore. It seemed to disturb Margaret that not even herself would talk to her friend about her Mum after she was gone. I love to talk about Margaret. Her friendship will always be one of the highlights of my life.

As Srini says it will be interesting to watch Francis grow up and assume of Margaret's characteristics. She will live on for Srini through Francis, who, by the way is already a very special personality.

I must bring myself to close for now, many many thanks again for your letter, Jo, and for your kind words. Being a friend to your sister has been the easiest and most natural thing I could ever do. Stay well and I hope we can keep in touch.

Love

Inge

A Happy Ending

After Maggie died and Srini was making a stab at getting his life back on track one of his friends suggested that he get someone in to help him look after Francis. A young German girl called Gertrud came to stay. Gertrud's role in all of this is a whole other story. Although she would never admit it, she was exactly what this little family in pain needed. She never met Maggie but she understood perfectly and intuitively what role she had to play. She provided security and nurture and a degree of discipline for the lost duo. She was young and yet with an enviable maturity. Time passed and Srini decided to move the family to Saskatoon and make a new start. He took a great interest in palliative care plus a few entrepreneurial adventures. Francis grew and eventually Srini thought to send him to Scotland for his senior education. He chose to send him to Loretto School in Musselburgh where several of his cousins were already studying.

Thomas Joseph Oliver Peter Francis John
(fine first cousins at Loretto)

69

This was such a brave move on Srini's part but it did mean that Francis was able to seal a relationship with his Scottish relatives and a bond was built that will never fade. While Francis was away at school Gertrud was pursuing her own career. She gained a university degree and was running a business in Toronto. She stayed in constant touch with Francis meeting him at the airport as he travelled to and fro from Scotland. When graduation day came at Loretto Srini asked Gertrud to attend as she was still so interested in her young charge. Srini had been on his own for long enough. These two people fell in love and decided to marry after all these years. My sister Mary attended their wedding and told me that as she sat in the chapel by herself she

Back row: Gertrud Erin Francis
Front row: Patrick Srini Brianna

had an incredible sense of Maggie's presence. Mary said it was the first time that she had had this feeling but that she hadn't imagined it. It was just a sense of approval and satisfaction. It has proved to be a fantastic match. Indeed at the time of writing Gertrud has been Srini's wife for twice as long as Maggie was. She is a fabulous wife and now mother to two little Charys. Francis at last has the family he has always longed for. He got married himself to Erin in August 06. The two families live happily in Calgary. It is a story that couldn't be made up and at its heart it has a young woman of beauty, brains and courage, my sister Maggie.

25th April 2007:
Email from Jo to her nephew Francis

Dear Francis,

How are things with you? Really looking forward to seeing you in the summer. I have emailed Srini today because things really are moving on now and I am pretty far forward with the book.

Please can you share with me some of your thoughts re the tape. What did you think/feel etc when you first heard it? Have you listened to it again or often? What made you decide to copy it out for the families? Anything you think might just add a little more to the story would be very helpful.

She made the tape first and foremost and only for you. I know that. It truly is a love story. However her words are so powerful when you think of it in connection with the bigger picture of life and love and loss and dealing with early death, that I think it will resonate with a much wider audience.

Talk to me.

Love as ever to you and Erin

Jo

25th April 2007: Email from Francis reflecting on first listening to the tape

From: Francis Chary

Sent: 25 April 2007 18:22

To: Jo Middlemiss

Subject: Re: From Jo

Dear Jo,

I'm doing really well. We're starting to settle into the house now, although we found out when we moved in that the previous owners were smokers. Quite a shock, I can tell you. We've been busy doing some small renos, such as painting the ceilings and washing the walls. Eventually, the plan is to rip out the carpet and install some hardwood, but we'll take that part slowly, I think. We don't want to get too ahead of ourselves.
I'm really looking forward to seeing all of you in the Summer, as well. We've got our flights and the hotel booked, so the only trick will be to rent the car to get up to... wait for it... Bedford. Yes, that's right, I know where I'm going now!
I've started to catch up a bit with all the cousins on facebook, which is really nice. I can't believe how they've changed! I suppose it's to be expected, but I remember Richard when he was just a little kid, and now... well, he's not small anymore.

So, on to the book and the tape.. First of all, let me say that I am dying to read it, and I fully support what you're doing. Having said that, I have to admit to you that I have only listened to the tape twice. Once with my Dad, and once with Erin. That was about 6 or 7 years ago. To be honest, I can't bear to put it in a tape player, it's just too hard for me to listen to. Now, don't think that I simply listened to the tape and put it out of my mind. Hearing my mother's voice, explaining one of the hardest things any person is ever likely to go through, was one of the most powerful events of my life. I may not be able to remember exactly what she said, but I have never forgotten what I believe she was telling me. I think about it all the time, and it has had a profound effect on me.

I was completely humbled by the grace and courage that she showed. I have wondered a great deal throughout my life what I would have done in a similar situation, and I can't say with any certainty that I could be so composed and strong.

How could I be like that? That's what I used to ask myself. How could I possibly find that strength, when everything was collapsing around me, to still laugh, and to still be able to think about life in a meaningful, positive way? Listening to her voice and words reinforced in my mind something that my Dad seems to have been trying to teach me all my life: That there is joy to be found in every part of life, every day, in even the smallest thing. I think that's the key, in the end. You can't lament what you've lost, you celebrate what you've had, and what you still have. It's that philosophy that I hope to live by for the rest of my life, and to hopefully pass on to my children. Copying the tape was probably the easiest decision I've ever made. After we heard it for the first time, my Dad and I immediately knew that it had to be distributed. Especially for you, her brothers and sisters, and for Nanie. I don't think she would have wanted it any other way. In some ways, you might be able to take even more out of it than I could, because you knew her so much better than I ever did. I knew you'd hear it and be thinking of how she looked, and what she was like back then. For me, it's a voice that comforts and a message that rings true, but I must admit, I don't have the same personal connection to it that I know you must. I wish I did, but it's hard. I have to imagine so much of who she was, and what she thought, so I wonder if it's not a very different experience for me, than it is for my Dad and you. Not in a bad way, just... different.

I'd really love to talk to you about it sometime. Do you think I could give you a call? Maybe on the weekend, if you're not busy?

I really appreciate you asking me. I hadn't thought about it much, mostly because I've been so busy with the new job, and moving, but I really would like to contribute in some way, if I could.

Talk to you soon!

Love,

Francis

Epilogue

A detailed reflection from Grown-up Francis, Maggie's child, 7 years after he first listened to it.

Listening to that tape for the first time was a revelation for me. I had heard my mother's voice before, but never in such quantity, and never in such a conversational tone. As the tape begins, she is speaking about her early life and her family (whom I know very well now). I don't know what she was hoping to accomplish when she started taping these segments for me, and I can't say for certain how she wanted it to sound. I think that when she started, she was hoping to have a great deal more time than she did.

The section about her life with the Dunn family is so easy to listen to, and always makes me smile. I can imagine two adults and seven children crammed with luggage into a tiny Beetle, and knowing my aunts and uncles, it must have been an adventure in itself just being in that car. It's so very interesting to learn that Papa (my grandfather) was meticulously organized, and fantastic that my mother mentions that this is in vast contrast to my father. She notes this difference casually, but it's crucially important to me. In addition to making me laugh out loud (because it's true, he's as disorganized as I am; I think it drives both Gertrud and Erin insane), it links my life and hers together in a very real way. Suddenly, this is not the recorded voice of someone whom I knew a very long time ago, but a person who I know intimately, through our shared connection with my Dad.

The beginning of the tape is very upbeat in tone, and I remember myself being so happy to listen to it. Hearing her describe Dunn birthdays (which I have been a part of, from time to time) lets me almost forget what I'm listening to, and just enjoy what she's saying.

It's not long until I'm brought back to Earth. In the next segment of the tape, she is in hospital on May 8th, having lost all feeling from the waist down. There is a clear difference in her voice; it is quite a bit weaker than before. Still, I'm struck by how calm and matter-of-fact she sounds as she records herself. It's not that she isn't bothered by what's happening, but it's clear that she has decided to simply get on with life, rather than feeling sorry for herself. It's humbling to hear, and I wonder if I could be so strong if I were in the same situation. The main thing she talks about in this segment is how a mother can explain the joy she feels about her child. I wonder about that question. Is it a question that many mothers ask themselves? Perhaps they do, but I would be willing to wager that very few ask that question so early in their child's life. It seems especially cruel to have to try and explain it to your son who is clearly not even old enough to understand what it means. Having said that, I'm glad she asked it on the tape, because I understand now what she was trying to say then.

On the 23rd of May, she had gone home from the hospital. In

the tape, she sounds sleepy, as though she is talking through a haze of medication. I believe at this point (although she never mentions it), her leg has been amputated, in an effort to stem the spread of the cancer. She mentions casually that she can't get from place to place, and has to be carried. She says this without a hint of self-pity or frustration in her voice, and I am again floored by her capacity for seeing the 'bigger picture'. I know that while she doesn't talk about it much, she had a tremendous faith in God, and I'm sure she believed very strongly that whatever purpose her situation served, it was part of a larger plan. My Dad dutifully raised me Catholic, as I believe they agreed. I may not have ended up in the same place spiritually as she did, but I have an enormous respect for what she believed, and am very grateful that she had her faith to help sustain her.

The end of her recording is very bizarre to me, to be honest. Hearing my own voice brings a host of questions: Is that me? Did I really sound like that? Am I really such a terrible singer? I like to think that I've improved since then. Again, the tone of the little singing lesson is very upbeat, and made me smile when I first heard it. When I listened to it for the first time, I really hoped that there would be more after it, that I would hear some other anecdotes about her life and what she thought about things. Sadly, she passed away soon after the last segment was recorded.

The fact that my mother passed away doesn't make me as sad

as one might think. I was so young when she died that my memories of her are not all that strong. I'm not even certain whether they are real memories, or whether I have constructed them from the stories I've heard about her, along with the fragmented pieces that swim up in my mind from time to time. What does make me sad on this tape is when I hear my Dad's voice, two weeks after she has passed away. If there is one thing I know very well in all this, it's the depth of feeling that my father had for my mother. I often think about how I would feel if I found out that my life with Erin was to be cut short. We have been married now for almost the same amount of time that my parents had been when the cancer was discovered. If I were to find out tomorrow that we only had months left together, I would be heartbroken, as my dad is on the tape. I can even hear my mother speaking through him and with him, when he says: "It was one of the saddest days of my life... but there you are; that's life". I think that the incredible strength of character that they both have is one of the biggest gifts in my life.

At this point I have to to wonder; what would life have been like had she not died? I don't mean to examine the implications of causality on today's reality. I'm not interested in asking how my whole life would have been different, as I am wonderfully happy with how my life has turned out so far. I simply wonder what our relationship would have been like. How would our personalities have meshed? Or perhaps even more interesting to ask; how would our personalities have clashed? Would she have been so sanguine about my Dad's lack of organization after being married to him for 10 years? Would she have tolerated the same behaviour in me? Knowing her brothers and sisters, I seriously doubt it. I think we would have had some fantastic fights, were she still with us. I think it goes without saying that we would have had great times, for the most part.

I think that in the final analysis, that's what I miss the most about her not being here. Whenever I ask about her, everyone always tells me what a wonderful person she was, how caring, how selfless, how thoughtful she was. I should first state that I am intensely proud of those things. However, nobody really talks about what made her angry. What her 'buttons' were. My regret is not having had the opportunity to find out. Whenever Erin and I go to my parents' house nowadays, we can end up talking for hours between the four of us. We have fantastic conversations, and can really generate great ideas amongst ourselves. Sometimes we make each other angry, but for the most part, we really enjoy each other's company. I wish I could have had that with my mother, as well. But, as they say, that's life. I am so fortunate for even having the opportunity to think of these things. Without her foresight in recording that tape for me, I would have never even thought to ask the question: "What was her least favourite food?"

Ultimately, I know my mother through other people. That's how it was for the first 18 years of my life, and I think that's how it will be for the rest of my life. Her thoughtfulness in creating this recording for me has enabled me to focus my questioning, and really get to the heart of who she was.

Maggie's words without any added information

Maggie in her own Words.
London, Ontario, Canada
30th April 1982

I'm sitting on the floor of our bedroom in 444

Belvedere Avenue in London, and I am just

wondering where you are, sitting listening to this, or

how old you are.

I am going to try and record a few things to you.

I thought of writing them down, I tried writing them

down, preparing it a little, but I think the best way will

be just to speak to you now and again until the tape is

finished.

Today is May.....no, it's not quite .

Today is the 30th of April, 1982.

It is a beautiful evening outside. It is about 7 o'clock and Daddy has just gone to collect some piece of furniture, or get it changed. You are across the road with Matthew and Megan, in 445 Belvedere Avenue and I hope you are having your supper there and I won't have to give it to you here.

May 1st:

Now it is May 1st and I am in the house on my own, waiting for you, ... you and your father to come home. Srini did buy a bed last night, an enormous bed, which I'm sure you still have in the house. It's a lovely one, but you had to go back to the shop 3 times, right across London, before he got the right parts for it. He was none too pleased, and neither were you, because you were waiting for your french fries to turn up and things

were being horribly delayed.

Francis Dear,

What should I tell you, that you might want to know

about me, or my life with your father,

and before your father?

Let me start with my own early days and then maybe

I'll talk about your early days

of which I've only seen a very few.

I was born, as I'm sure you know, in Glasgow in Scotland

and I was number...... fifth in a family of seven.

There were eight originally but one died early, after birth.

We lived in a fairly large house in Glasgow.

Both Nanie and Papa were doctors, as you know, and they struggled. Seven children, I don't think, was ever an easy thing. It was never an easy thing to make ends meet with seven children, but they managed very well. We were a happy bunch. We all used to go on holidays together and I would say we got on very well as a family, and we still do up until this day.

I don't think there is one of us who wouldn't travel a long way to see the other if they were in trouble.

What else? I think I was a fairly quiet and shy child. Maybe, being fifth in line you didn't get a chance to get to say many things, so I probably just kept quiet a good deal of the time.

I was reasonably industrious at school. I did quite well without trying too hard.

And, I took music lessons, violin lessons, as you will see by the violin that's left for you.
We all did, we all took violin and piano lessons. Some fell by the wayside. In fact most fell by the wayside, we didn't really make much of it but we learned anyway.

And then school.
I think school for me was a pretty uneventful kind of time, and I don't remember too much about it. It certainly wasn't unhappy, but I don't remember it with any terrific enthusiasm.

I left school when I was sixteen and I went straight into Glasgow University then, to do medicine. And that was a fine time. I enjoyed that. Again, I stayed at home then.....It was a rigorous kind of course. You had to work fairly hard. I was young and not too confident, so I probably overdid it, and and didn't enjoy university life to the full, but perhaps many people say that. Maybe if I had my time again I wouldn't do it any different. However I finished university and I felt then definitely that I was going to spread my wings, and I looked around for a job outside Glasgow. And I found one as a house surgeon in Leicester in England, and that's where I met your dad.

How am I doing so far?

I seem to have reached the age of 23 without telling you very much. Would you be interested in maybe what kind of things we did when we were kids? We used to go amazing holidays. Papa, my father, was the best organiser in the world.

He used to be packing the car, preparing to pack the car, weeks ahead of the holiday. I would say, almost in direct contrast to Srini, your own father, who would be packing, (he would get it all done mind you the night before. Shove it in!)

But Papa was meticulous. Everything had to be right. And when you think about it, to get nine people going on holiday in a V.W. Beetle, you had to do a bit of thinking. And that's what we did. We used to

go on holiday in a Beetle. I don't even know if they

are still around .I don't think they make them anymore,

certainly not in Germany. But we did.

There was two in the back cubby hole, four in the

back seat, and my Mother and Father and the baby

Bernard in the front. (she sniffs) Excuse me. And

the whole car would be packed up to the hilt. We were

allowed one small plastic bag with our clothes in and

that was it. No extras. But it was great fun. We had

some.....we had some fantastic holidays. We used to go

to St Andrews in Scotland, we used to go to Girvan

and we used to go to Ireland.

I don't think we ever went, no, we never went abroad as a family, we just used to........., it was just too much and probably too expensive. Anyway we enjoyed that kind of thing. We had great, a lot of good times as a family. We used to have.....the birthdays....the birthdays were an exercise. Everyone at the birthday had to make a speech about the person whose birthday it was. So you would go round the whole family saying what do you think about this person.

Well we used to be fairly.......I was shy at them all, all I used to say was "Happy Birthday, I hope you have a nice time." But the boys, Johnny and Frank, Bernard and Gerard were so...., as the years went by they got funnier and funnier.

Oh I think, yes you're home, so is Daddy. I can hear you coming in the back door.

O.K. I will just pause just now

Mags: Francis

Francis: Yep

Mags: Are you coming? Would you like to hear yourself on the tape? Hello, hello, Francis what have you been doing?

the tape's on, the tape's on . Say hello to yourself.

Francis: Eh

Mags: Hello Francis, say hello Francis!

Srini: Hi Francis

May 8th: Recorded in Hospital

Francis , the date is now May the 8th. And over the last few days my health has gone down again and I have had to come into hospital. I have lost the power in my legs, my right leg, and probably from the waist down. I can't move very well. I didn't intend or plan to talk to you too much about this cancer that I've had and that Srini and I have had to deal with for the last two years. More or less since you've been born. But here I am in this situation where it has suddenly hit me and Srini again and you now. Once again, we don't really know exactly what is going to happen, or when. So I am just going to talk to you whenever I feel like it, whenever I can, and try to give you some idea of what it all means to us.

You, Francis, since you've been born, have never given us any cause but for great joy, apart from a few odd nights when you wouldn't go to sleep. You have been......well...you've just been part of us since we've been together and married. We knew you were coming about three months after we were married, and immediately you were part of our lives and as so you are now, and such a joyous part and happy part of our lives.

How does a mother explain to you what a wonderful joy it is to have you around?

I'll pause there for a moment Francis.

May: Recorded in hospital a few days later

Anybody listening to our story of our life over the last few years, may think how sad, what a sad tale it all is, that a young family, very happy, should lose one of its members fairly early on in life. And we've seen it that way too. ......how sad it is, we possibly can't spend much more time together.

Well, Francis I can only say, that there's been so many moments of sheer joy in the time that I have spent with your father, and in the time that we've spent together with you. I don't know or I can't think that many people could have had more happy moments than we have had. I am sure in the years to come, Francis, you and your daddy will have clashes, disagreements, arguments, but the love and the bond that I see between you both now, will never be lost. It really is an impossible task to say in words the meaning of the life, albeit short, that I have had with Srini. He is the most wonderful man to be loved by and to love. And I simply thank God that I have had the opportunity in my life to be in this position, of giving and receiving such a love.

Francis,

Perhaps this is not a bad time to mention, or speak about a few things that are close to my heart. In the way of God, Christ, religion. I certainly believe in God's hand having an effect in life. I can't say I understand the meaning of all the things that happen, why they happen, why they should happen to us. But in all this time, I have never felt bitter, or why should this have happened to me. I feel more,

why not? It's happened to others, its part of life, of

living, and its more important how these things affect

you rather than why did they affect you. The most

concrete evidence, or surely not evidence, but the

most strongest feeling I have had during all this time

is one of the tremendous power and influence of

the Good Lord in everything. The fact that I can

be here talking to you on the tape, this is wonderful.

The kind of support, and love, and encouragement

we've had as a family, from my family, from Srini's

family is immeasurable. And the wonderful feelings

and emotions which this has inspired in us is again

something, which I think, perhaps, not many people

experience in their lives.

May 23rd: Home from Hospital

Darling Francis,

I have moved onto a new day. It's almost the end of May. May 23rd I think it is. I am home from hospital, and such a joy it is to be home too. Oh! You would be surprised at the organization in this room where I am lying, in my bed, talking to you. Mary, your Aunt Mary, your godmother, is here and Nanie and Bernard. Just helping out, looking after me. I suppose the biggest difference for me now, since going into hospital this time, is I can no longer get myself from A to B, so I have to be carried. And that's probably the only difference, and it doesn't bother me too much and it doesn't seem to bother anybody else. So I usually spend most of my time in the room here in the morning, then get up and go into the front room and stay there for some time. And that's more or less the order of the day, sounds boring doesn't it. Well its not.

O.K. Francis.

Lets see if I can tell you what you are up to these days. Even in two short weeks, I come home and you are talking more. Asking "What?" "Why?" after every sentence. Running around. Still won't go to bed at night ......but we don't mind. What else do you do? There's a boy across the road, Matthew of course, your buddy; most of the day you spend your time trying to get over to see Matthew and Megan, which you do successfully.

You certainly have a mind of your own these days, and I suppose that's just about right.

Srini's words, ending as the tape runs out.
Spoken two weeks after Maggie's death.

O.K. Francis,

That's the last you'll hear of Mama now. I think its

been about two weeks since she has passed away and

I told you that she has gone to God. You saw Mama

and we went to the service. Monsignor Roney came

to the house to say the prayers. Mama was laid out

in the house for two nights, and lots of friends came

to see her. Nanie and Papa were here, so was Frank

at the service. After the service Mama was taken

away to the crematorium and we went to the chapel

there as well. It was one of the saddest days of my

life, that's life. I can't tell you how much I loved your

Mama, I know I'll miss her. I'll tell you more about her

anyway, in the future. This is just to let you know what

I thought about her. She was the best friend I had.
Maybe she will be around and talk to us, if not talk
to us, just guide us in whatever we are doing. Nanie
and Papa are going away to Glasgow and you will go
to Glasgow with them. Then I will probably work for
a few months and then bring you back home. My plan
is to look after you. At least I see your Mama in you.
O.K. I don't think nothing is going to happen to me,
but if anything happens to me, I'm sure either Johnny
and Carol or Josephine and Andy or Servotham
and Salochanan, one of these three will look after
you. Life is funny though. You really want some things
in life and you go and search for them and you find
them........(the tape ends)

Jo Middlemiss grew up in Glasgow but moved to Berlin to teach the children of the Armed Forces Personnel. That was where she met her husband Andy and travelled with him throughout his service career. They have three grown up sons and live in Angus in Scotland. As well as writing for various publications she is a Personal Life Coach, Relationship Counsellor and Development Trainer. Her coaching business is called Dreamzwork.

jomiddlemiss@dreamzwork.co.uk